THE Pasto᷄
UNAUTHORIZED
INSTRUCTION
BOOK

"What Every Church Leader Ought to Know"

by R. Michael and Rebecca Sanders

Abingdon Press / Nashville

THE PASTOR'S UNAUTHORIZED INSTRUCTION BOOK

MANUFACTURED IN THE UNITED STATES OF AMERICA

To the late Reverend Frederick "Crocodile Freddy" Durkin,
a man with a true pastor's heart.
What more need be said?

This collection could not have been conceived and written
without the help of the
Seven Parishes of Illinois,
those places we have served.
They were often wonderful and brutal.

1

Always speak in positive or neutral terms about former pastors — no matter what kind of twits they were.

2

Never criticize the memorial plaques —
even if they are bigger than the pew.

3

Be cautious about the people who first gush over you as a new pastor — it is often a guilt reflex over the poor treatment they gave the last pastor.

4

Get what you can in writing.

5

It takes about two years for you and your church to get to know each other. Then it takes a year or so to get over it.

6

Never take on a job around the church "just until we find someone" unless you are willing for the job to be yours for the duration.

7
Being young doesn't make someone a good youth leader.

8
Drink kool-aid and eat cookies with the Bible School kids.

9

Don't preach to the people at church about the poor
attendance — they are there.

10
Keep a prayer journal.

11

Don't be afraid to preach a good sermon many times —
just do it for different crowds.

12

Never claim, even by subtle omission of facts, that
a borrowed illustration is original.

13
Read your Bible in a number of translations.

14
Don't fight battles over the color of the carpet.

15
Don't chair meetings.

16

Give consistently to your church. Someone notices
and tells others if you don't.

17

Have a designated time every year to discuss your
compensation.

18

Never, NEVER accept "Gee pastor, things are tight right now," as an excuse for no raise. Things are always tight in a church.

19

Get and use an answering machine.

20

Return all calls — even if the caller says you don't have to.

21

Read the "pop" Christian books you despise as shallow. Some of your people will.

22

For the same reason, watch some Christian television.

23
Be part of an accountability group.

24

Make friends with pastors you can trust
— there will be those you can't.

25

You be a pastor other pastors can trust.

26
Your family comes before your church.

27

Take ALL vacations. Put two weeks together because
the real vacation happens that second week.

28

Take your days off — most of the time.

29

Listen politely to the patriarchs and matriarchs of the church even if they are busybodies and dullards.

30

The longer you listen, the smarter they become.

31
Learn elementary Greek.

32
Learn elementary Hebrew.

33

If your theology allows you to drink alcoholic beverages, reconsider it for your people's sake.

34

Some people will tell you
it doesn't matter if you visit certain shut-ins.
Watch these people,
they will lie about other things as well.

35

Try to have a paid professional at the piano —
you can expect more from them.

36

Never hire custodial help from within the church membership.

37
You get what you pay for — especially in carpets and sound equipment.

38
Buy furniture that can coordinate with the ubiquitous puke gold carpet and beige walls of parsonages.

39

Buy the new car before you go to the next church.

40

Go over repairs and improvements to the parsonage
before you come. Memories become shadowy when the
new pastor arrives.

41

Resist the temptation to catalogue the sheep and the goats
in your congregation.

42

Don't look down on those who are only occasional
attenders — they may be the smart ones.

43

Read C. S. Lewis — including his children's stories.

44

Don't be telling people "what the real Greek says."

45

Eat with gusto and seconds at church socials.

46

Smile when you have to preach a negative sermon.

47

Never use your last sermon to settle the score. It won't.

48
Professionals often keep time sheets — do it.

49

Turn off your phone for meals and other family times.
Trust me.

50

Remember to turn the phone back on.

51

Sing with enthusiasm even if you know what you sound like.

52

Never expect payment for weddings or funerals.

53

Never refuse payment for a wedding or funeral for
pious reasons — it's rude.

54
Attend grade and high school band and chorus concerts.

55
Go to some local ball games — but behave.

56

Miss that important town council meeting if a church member needs you elsewhere.

57
Hold hands with your spouse in public.

58

Learn how to give a gratifying Mother's Day sermon.

59

Never endorse criticism of a church member by an ex-member even if it sounds plausible.

60

Learn to do something new every year.

61
Read non-**theological** books.

62
Take a secular magazine — excepting *Playboy* of course.

63

Be a friend to pastors of other denominations and traditions — the Lord's vineyard is vast.

64
Never compromise on moral or theological issues.

65
Compromise on anything else.

66

Don't go back to a former pastorate to officiate
at weddings or funerals — be an honored guest instead.

67
Talk to, not at, the youth. Better yet, listen a lot.

68
Do children's sermons every week.

69
Never preach children's sermons to the parents.

70

Learn your people's names early. Take a course,
learn a system, but do it.

71

Always leave the parsonage spotless when you move.

72
Double check that all bills are paid.

73
Never handle any money of the church. Never.

74

Keep regular office hours if only a few.

75

When you get the call at ten in the morning and they ask,
"Did I wake you pastor?"
resist the temptation for a cute remark.

76

Resist the temptation for cute and flip remarks
to all stupid questions.

77

Remember, there are some in the congregation who think pastors really don't work. Learn to handle it graciously and without apologies or explanations.

78

Don't give a job to a committee when an individual can do it.

79

Don't put people on committees to shut them up —
unless it is a committee without real power or function.
There should be several of those.

80

If you make a pastoral visit and no one is home, leave them a card or a note. They will appreciate your effort.

81
Don't spend more time trying to activate inactive members
than you do looking for new members.

82
Don't make major changes right away.
YOU are a major change.

83
Beauty and excellence need no explanations.

84
Tape your services and listen.

85
Eat right.

86
Exercise regularly.

87
Get proper rest.

88

Ignore the idiots who say
they would rather burn out than rust out.
You stay for the long haul.

89
Have regular medical check-ups.

90
You are the finest tool you have for doing ministry.

91
Write thank-you notes frequently.

92
Praise people, lots of people.

93

Keep tabs on your people.
They can slip away unnoticed so easily.

94
Even if you don't need the raise the next pastor will.

95
A church that treats its pastor cheaply may have learned to do so from earlier pastors. Don't you compound the sin.

96

Check into your state's law concerning
worker's compensation and pastors.

97

Hire bright, energetic people.

98

Check your church's insurance coverage — especially what they carry on the parsonage.

99

Make sure your church meets state and local building codes.

100

Make your church "handicapped accessible."

101
Get pew Bibles so you can all read
the Scripture together sometimes.

102
Failing this, print your text in the bulletin.

103

Check the lighting in the sanctuary for the reading of small Bible print.

104
Join into community activities.

105
Learn to read dramatically.

106
Print high quality bulletins. Find a printer
or get the use of a laser-printer.

107
Get a plain paper copier.

108

Leave your itinerary for the day with your spouse
if your spouse will be answering the phone.

109

Leave an extra key to church with your spouse or responsible children when you are gone.

110
Have your children live up to your expectations
— not the church's.

111
Don't require your children to attend ALL church functions.

112
Have a pet.

113
Have green, living things in your office.

114

Buy the most reliable vehicle you can honestly afford.
You will live in it.

115

Take your spouse out on a regular basis without children
and to non-church functions.

116

Get a Rolodex — or **maintain** addresses on your computer.

117

Call ahead on hospital visits because they sometimes discharge surprisingly early.

118
Get an appointment book or a "personal digital assistant."

119
Look at it every morning.

120

Be among the first to welcome a new pastor to town.

121

Try not to be topical every Sunday in your preaching —
it wears thin.

122
Shake hands firmly in church, but gently with the elderly.

123
Shake hands with the children, too.

124

In small communities frequent local businesses
even if it costs you more.

125
Go to other church's chili suppers.

126
Take local newspapers.

127
Bank at local banks.

128
Lose that extra fifteen pounds — now!

129
Never brag too much on how good your last church was.

130
Never complain about how bad your last church was.

131
Don't take people's reactions personally.

132

Never use a church as your stepping stone to bigger and better things. There aren't any.

133
Listen carefully to elder pastors.

134
Never call an elder pastor by their first name
unless they ask you to.

135

Be carefully aware of who and how you hug church members — it's a sad time out there.

136

If possible have a private telephone line to your home.

137
Never counsel someone where you two are alone.

138
Never violate 137. Never.

139
Know your limitations — refer, refer, refer.

140

Listen to the popular Christian music
no matter what your preference is.

141
Listen to secular stations on occasion.

142
Travel.

143

Pastors cannot take stay at home vacations.

144

When on vacation, give a number where you can be reached to one or two very responsible people.

145
Take continuing education courses.

146
Teach a course at your local Community College.

147

If someone gives you a tape to listen to or something to read and you agree — do it and do it immediately.

148

There will be those in all churches who will always support you as pastor. Bless them and pray for them often.

149
The longer pastorate is usually the more effective.

150
For some strange reason, the third year
seems to be the hardest.

151

If you leave tomorrow, the church will still be there.

152
Keep your zipper zipped.

153

Don't over-react if there is public criticism of your spouse or children.

154
Never condone public criticism of spouse or children —
Your promise of "until death do we part" was not
to the church.

155
Learn the local history.

156
Travel locally. Learn where all the quaint little towns
and places are.

157

Leave the parsonage better than you found it.
Plant fruit trees or rose bushes.

158

If the parsonage doesn't have a fence,
have the church put one up.
Robert Frost was right.

159
Put some meaningful books in the church library.

160
Have a theological question and answer night on a regular basis.

161

Never take a critic's word on a new translation or hymnal.
Find out yourself.

162
Read Calvin Miller's *The Singer*.

163
Read D. Bonhoeffer's *Life Together*.

164

Make sure your church has counseling liability insurance.

165

Do a weekly radio program at least once in your ministry.

166

Make some real friends within your congregation.

167

Take snap shots of church events and post them.

168
Turn off the TV often.

169

Learn the difference between a Pentecostal, a Charismatic, and a member of a Third Wave Church.

170

Find ways to celebrate the small victories
in the life of the church.

171

Once in a while, return to former churches
for their homecomings.

172

If invited, go to those 25th and 50th wedding anniversaries
occurring in your church.

173

If you are new to the rural setting,
discover what they mean by oysters before you eat.

174
Learn the stories behind the hymns.

175

Read C. S. Lewis' *Screwtape Letters* and believe.

176

Collect a book of your own favorite sermons.

177

Learn the difference between a Fundamentalist and a Conservative.

178
When people compliment your sermon,
a simple thank-you is sufficient.

179
Someone will compliment any sermon.

180

Write letters to friends — they're too expensive to waste.

181
Keep in touch with seminary and college friends.

182

Be well groomed even if you are only going to the corner convenience store.

183
Leave a gift to the church.

184
If you have a staff, let them do their job.

185
Never let people sin easily.

186

Most people who get angry at you aren't.
They're mad at God and life.

187
Read the poetry of Carl Sandburg.

188
Write a column for your local newspaper.

189
Read, Read, Read!

190
Talking too much is an occupational hazard.

191
Write your own lyrics to the great hymns.

192

Don't always tell people what you do for a living right away.
Let them actually get to know you.

193
Sit on your porch.

194

There are those who will try to take advantage of you and the church.

195

Sometimes, allow them to take advantage.

196
Convince your church to adopt a seminarian.

197
If your church won't adopt a seminarian, you do it.

198
Be ready for the "why" questions.
You won't always have a good answer, but be ready.

199
Have a children's pageant every year.

200

Fight any effort to put the church's money into savings or into a Certificate of Deposit — unless it is for a specific cause and not just for "a rainy day."

201

Read *A Severe Mercy* by Sheldon Vanauken.

202
Don't depend exclusively on your denomination's retirement program.

203

If you say you will, do it no matter the cost.

204

If you are asked to speak in public outside your church,
cut out five to ten minutes of the time
you think you should take.

205

Resist the temptation to sell insurance part-time.

206

If you get to the point when you feel that you are fed up
with the church and are ready to quit,
give yourself three months and during that time
read *What's Right With the Church* by William Willimon.

207

I've never heard a pastor criticized for listening too much.

208
Use your Greek and Hebrew on a regular basis.

209
Add new reference books to your personal library regularly.

210
Take a liberal Christian publication.

211
Take a conservative Christian publication.

212

It is easier to get forgiveness than permission.

213
Stay away from credit cards.

214

If you borrow a book, return it promptly.
Pastors are notorious book thieves.

215
Write enthusiastic letters to the editor
about the issues you care about.

216
Don't write knee-jerk reaction letters to the editor.

217
Trade pulpits with other pastors for a Sunday.

218
Be suspicious of those pastors who won't trade.

219
Never delight in the schism or break-up of other churches.

220
Do not actively seek new members from disgruntled factions in other churches.

221

As a general rule, preach only your sermons.
Canned or bought sermons cheat you and your congregation.

222

Read other sermons, learn from them,
even "steal" from them, but don't preach them.

223

Rent and watch the movie *Places in the Heart*.
Meditate on the final scene.

224

If your sermon is over thirty minutes, cut it.

225

If there is nothing you can cut, make it a two part sermon and finish it that night or next week.

226

Don't eat a big or heavy meal just before you preach.

227

Without violating church bylaws,
avoid voting as much as possible.

228

Arrive at office and for services early.

229
Don't complain. Fix it or forget it.

230
Never criticize other pastors.

231
Remember, the church will be there long after you are not.

232
To the church you are, sadly, expendable. To your family you are not.

233

The parsonage belongs to the church, but it is your home.

234

Be sensitive to the church's outmoded ways of doing things.
They accomplished a lot before you were ordained.

235

You will learn certain special ways your church operates
that are different from the rest.
Write this down for the next pastor.

236

Don't editorialize on what you write down.

237
Many pastors resign late Sunday night or early Monday morning.

238
Most "re-up" by Tuesday.

239

Read the journals of the great Christians, such as John Wesley.

240

Be courteous and professional in your dealings with your local funeral home.

241

Keep funeral sermons short.

242

Let the Boy Scouts and Girl Scouts use your facilities.

243
Never interrupt a sermon
to personally quiet or discipline children.

244
Never use the pulpit to single out individuals for criticism.

245

When you read the Christmas story to your church,
use the King James Version.

246

Talk to your spouse about what is going on in the church
— good or bad.

247

Don't expect to be treated fairly in the ministry.
No one else is.

248
Don't talk about church problems
in front of your small children.

249

Halve the promises people make to you
when you first go to a church.

250

Be proud of your denominational heritage, but remember:
God allows denominations to exist
because of the hardness of our hearts.

251

Develop a thick skin about the joke that people make about preachers who only work a couple hours each week.

252

Never send your resume out on Monday morning.

253

Unless you are really, REALLY sure,
never go to a church for less money.

254
Don't resign until you have somewhere to go.

255
Ignore unsigned letters.

256
Never get into heated discussion on the phone. Tell them you will meet them somewhere in person and work it out.

257
Despite your brilliant and inspired insight,
the canon of Scripture is closed.

258
Never go to a hastily called board or deacon's meeting
without a friend.

259
Never threaten to resign in order to get your way.

260
Sometimes victory is yours
not because of your brilliant rhetoric or convincing argument,
but by simply surviving the battle.

261
If it is that bad, merely resign with dignity.

262
If you are having real trouble with an individual,
pick a neutral site to meet. Bring a friend.

263
You should bring a friend but not a tape recorder.

264

Most people problems are misunderstandings
based on a faulty definition of terms.

265

Read to your children at bedtime.

266

One day you will be that pastor
about whom your people are always bragging.

267

Never invite back a singing group that says during their
program, "We don't know this song too well,
so just listen to the words."

268

There will always be someone in the wedding party who thinks he or she can do it better than you can.

269

If a conflict arises over procedure at a wedding rehearsal, clearly and loudly remind the bride and groom it is their wedding and ask them what they want.

270

If the couple wants to write part of the ceremony,
insist on seeing it long before rehearsal night.

271
Fill out all documentation for the wedding
before the actual ceremony.

272

Buy or borrow a word processor and learn how to use it.
MACs are the best.

273

When someone in the church has a moral failure, help them confess it and get on with life. Don't be one that makes them defend an action they already know is wrong.

274

Avoid any youth activity that is labeled with the word "lock-in." Trust me.

275

Invite the youth group to your house for pizza sometime. Worry about the mess later.